WILLIAM BLAKE

The Tyger

ILLUSTRATED BY

Neil Waldman

HARCOURT BRACE & COMPANY

San Diego   New York   London

Requests for permission to make
copies of any part of the work should be mailed to:
Permissions Department,
Harcourt Brace & Company, 6277 Sea Harbor Drive,
Orlando, Florida 32887-6777.

Library of Congress Cataloging-in-Publication Data
Blake, William, 1757–1827.
The tyger/by William Blake; illustrated by Neil Waldman. — 1st ed.
p.   cm.
Summary: An illustrated version of Blake's well-known poem,
viewing the "tyger, tyger, burning bright,
in the forests of the night."
ISBN 0-15-292375-6
1. Tigers — Juvenile poetry.   2. Children's poetry, English.
[1. Tigers — Poetry.   2. English poetry.]   I. Waldman, Neil, ill.
II. Title.
PR4144.T9   1993
821'.7 — dc20   92-23378

BCDEF

The illustration in this book was done in acrylics on canvas.
The display type was set in Noris Script by Thompson Type, San Diego, California.
The text type was set in Cloister and Noris Script by Thompson Type, San Diego, California.
Color separations by Bright Arts, Ltd., Singapore
Printed and bound by Tien Wah Press, Singapore
Production supervision by Warren Wallerstein and Ginger Boyer
Design by Trina Stahl
Art direction by Michael Farmer

PRINTED IN SINGAPORE

For Jeri,
my loving and caring friend,
confidante, partner, and teacher

— N. W.

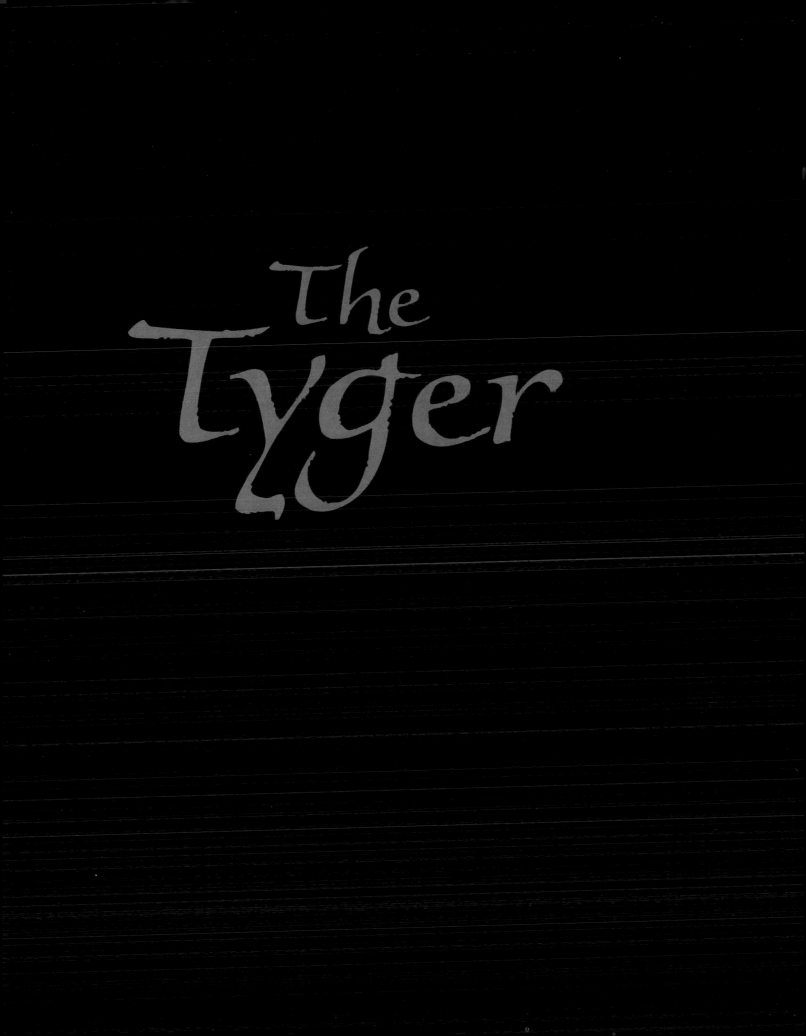

Tyger Tyger,
    burning bright,
In the forests
    of the night;

What immortal
hand or eye
Could frame thy
fearful symmetry?

In what distant

    deeps or skies

Burnt the fire

    of thine eyes?

On what wings
    dare he aspire?
What the hand,
    dare seize the fire?

And what shoulder,
and what art,
Could twist the sinews
of thy heart?

And when thy heart
began to beat,
What dread hand?
And what dread feet?

What the hammer?
What the chain,
In what furnace
was thy brain?

What the anvil?
   What dread grasp,
Dare its deadly
   terrors clasp?

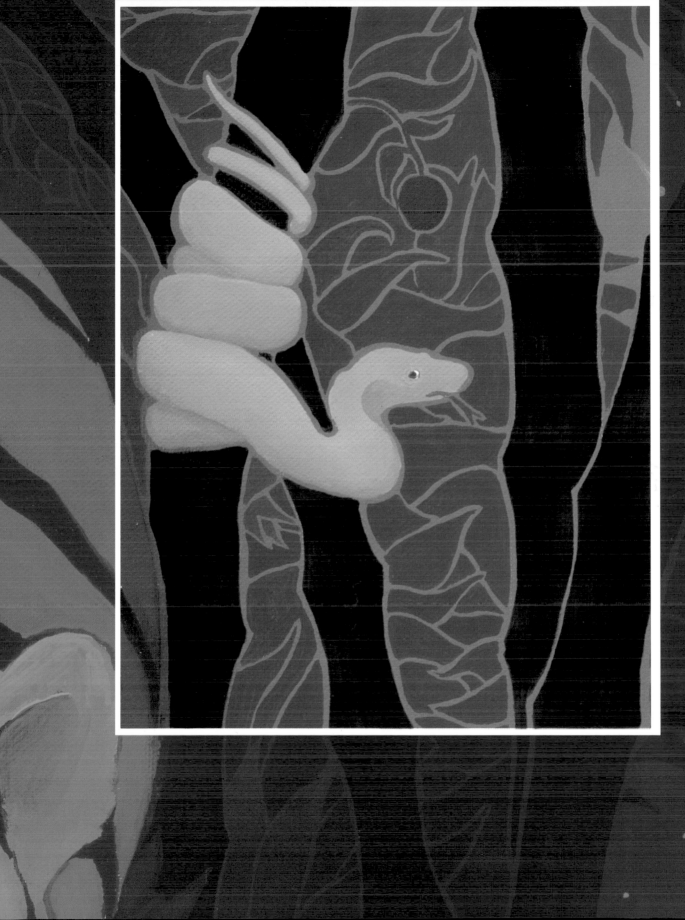

When the stars
threw down their spears
And water'd heaven
with their tears:

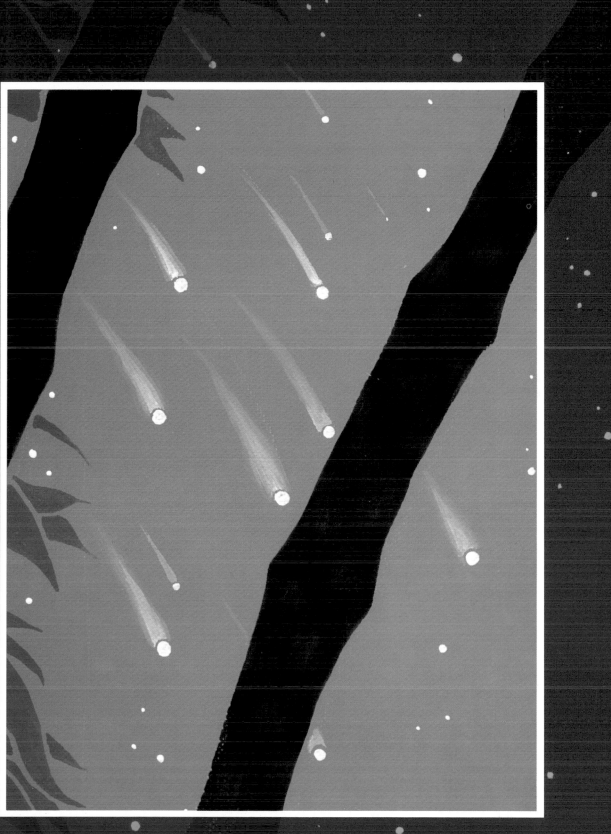

Did he smile
his work to see?
Did he who made
the Lamb make thee?

Tyger Tyger,
    burning bright,
In the forests
    of the night:

What immortal
hand or eye
Dare frame thy
fearful symmetry?